THE SPRING FEASTS

Activity Book for Beginners

Bible Pathway
— Adventures®

The Spring Feasts Activity Book for Beginners

Bible Pathway Adventures® is a trademark of BPA Publishing Ltd.
Defenders of the Faith® is a trademark of BPA Publishing Ltd.

ISBN: 978-1-98-858593-2

Author: Pip Reid
Creative Director: Curtis Reid

For free Bible resources including coloring pages, worksheets, puzzles and more, visit our website at:

www.biblepathwayadventures.com

Introduction for Parents

Your children will LOVE learning about the Spring Feasts with The Spring Feasts Activity Book for Beginners. Packed with coloring pages, worksheets, crafts and puzzles to help educators just like you teach children the Biblical faith. Includes scripture references for easy Bible verse look-up. The perfect discipleship resource for Sabbath and Sunday School lessons, and homeschooling.

Bible Pathway Adventures® helps educators teach children the Biblical faith in a fun and creative way. We do this via our illustrated storybooks, Activity Books, and printable activities - available for download on our website www.biblepathwayadventures.com

Thanks for buying this Activity Book and supporting our ministry. Every book purchased helps us continue our work providing free Classroom Packs and discipleship resources to missions and families around the world.

The search for Truth is more fun than Tradition!

★BONUS★

Our illustrated The Risen King storybook is available for download.
Type the link into your browser to get your FREE copy today!
https://BookHip.com/ZNJVLP

Table of Contents

Feast of First Fruits (Bikkurim)

Day of Pentecost (Shavu'ot)

Crafts & Projects

This book belongs to:

....

Draw something

Feast of Unleavened Bread

When the Israelites left Egypt, they were in such a hurry that they did not have time to let their bread dough rise. They carried the unbaked dough on their backs, and as they were walking, it cooked in the sun. Because the bread had no yeast, it became hard and flat, and was known as 'matzah'. Eating matzah every year during the Feast of Unleavened Bread reminds us of the Israelites' escape from Egypt and how Yah delivered them from slavery.

The Feast of Unleavened Bread begins on the fifteenth day of Nissan (March - April) with the Passover meal, and lasts for seven days. The Passover points to Yeshua as our Passover lamb. Yeshua died on the day of preparation for the Passover at the same hour the lambs were being killed for the Passover meal that evening.

Color the door!

"These are the Appointed Times of Yah, holy convocations which you shall proclaim at their appointed times."
Leviticus 23:4

🌿 The king of Egypt 🌿

When the Hebrews lived in Egypt, Pharaoh was the king. Trace the words. Color the picture.

The king of Egypt

Where is Egypt?

The Hebrews lived in the land of Egypt for many years.
Color Egypt green. Color the water blue.

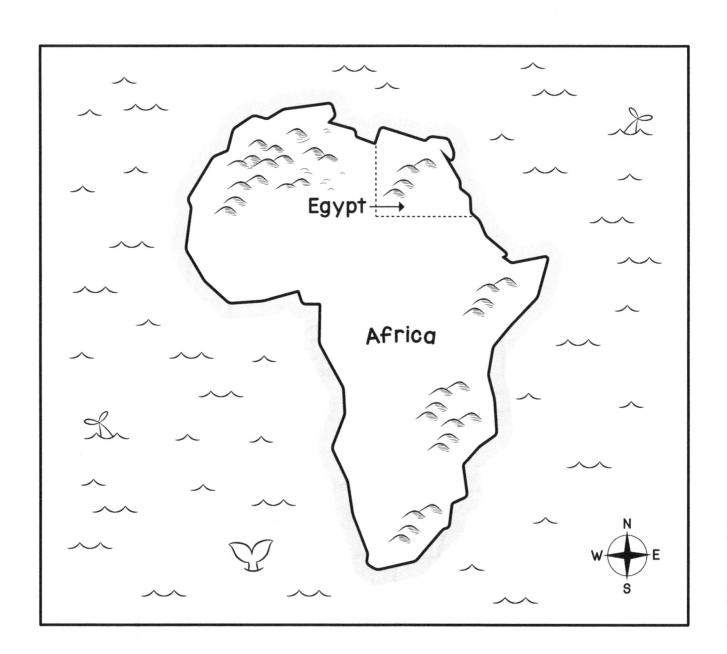

E is for Egypt

Moses was born in the land of Egypt.
Trace the letters and words. Color the picture.

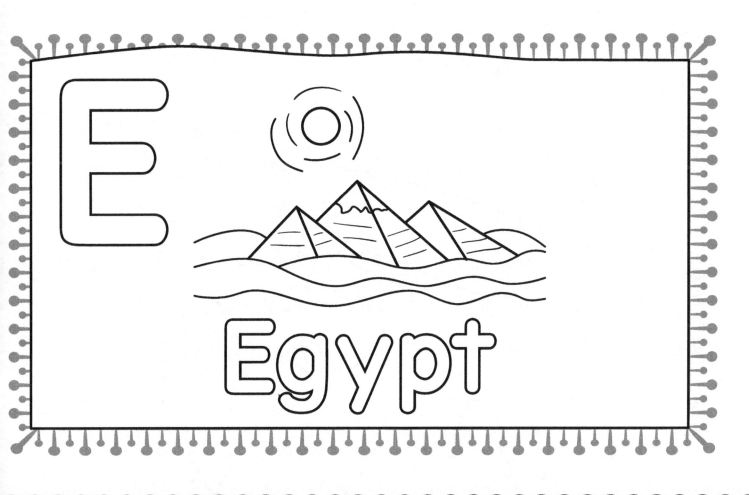

E is for Egypt

Moses

Moses grew up in the land of Egypt.
Connect the dots to see the picture.

🌿 What's different? 🌿

Circle the picture that is different.

The Ten Plagues

What a lot of plagues!
Count them and write the number in the box.

blood

locust

hail

lice

cow

boils

frog

death of firstborn

fly

darkness

🌿 Trace the Words 🌿

Color the pictures.

blood

frog

lice

fly

🌿 Trace the Words 🌿

Color the pictures.

cow

boils

hail

locust

✣ Trace the Words ✣

Color the pictures.

Plague of frogs

Yah filled the Nile River with frogs. This was the second plague. Connect the dots to see the picture.

Yah's Passover instructions

In the land of Egypt, Yah told the Hebrews how to eat
the Passover meal. Trace the words.
Color the pictures.

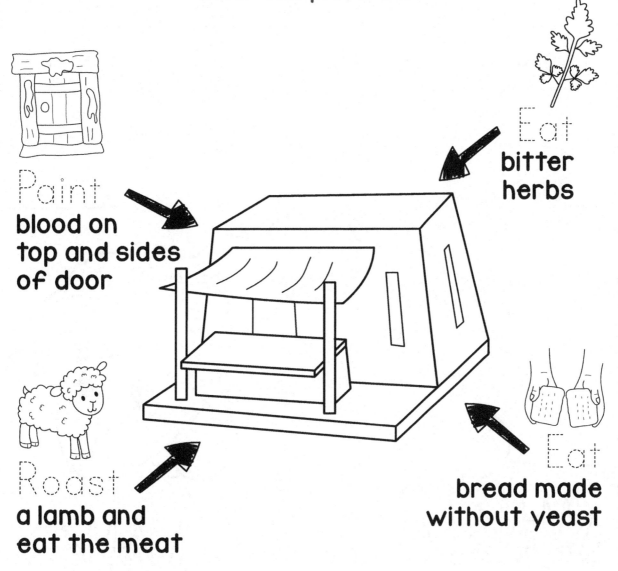

Paint
blood on top and sides of door

Eat
bitter herbs

Roast
a lamb and eat the meat

Eat
bread made without yeast

The Passover lamb

The Hebrews obeyed Yah's instructions.
They ate a lamb for the Passover meal.
Can you follow instructions like the Hebrews?
Use the color code to finish the picture.

1 = grey	2 = black	3 = blue	4 = white

❧ Fast and slow ❧

Yah told the Israelites to eat the Passover meal in a hurry. This means they had to eat the food as fast as possible! What moves fast? What moves slow? Draw two objects in the boxes below.

Fast

Slow

❧ How to eat the Passover ❧

Educators: Read Exodus 12:11 (ESV) with your children.
Yah told the Israelites how to eat the Passover meal.
What were His instructions? Color the items
mentioned in this Bible passage.

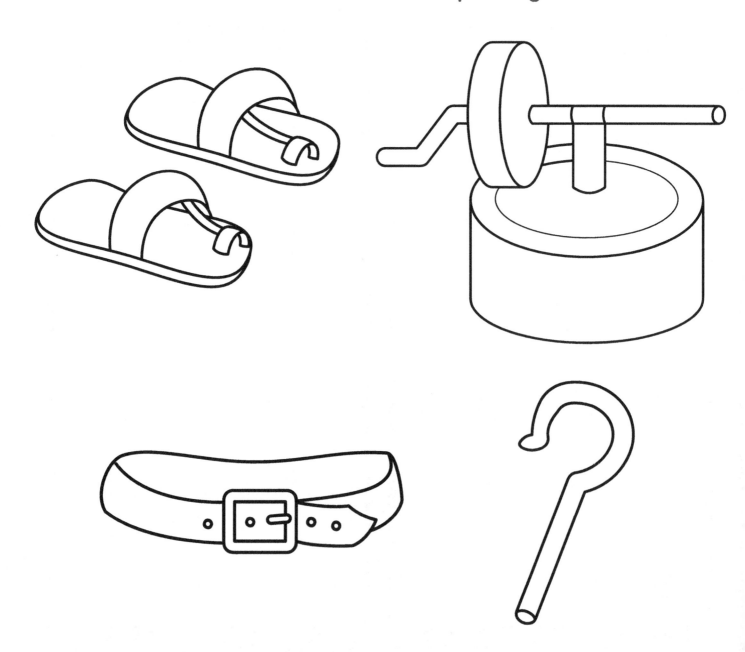

The Passover

🌿 The Passover 🌿

Yah told the Israelites to put lamb's blood
on the top and sides of their doorways.
Draw blood on the top and sides of the door.

The Passover Meal

What do you eat for the Passover meal?
Draw the food you eat.

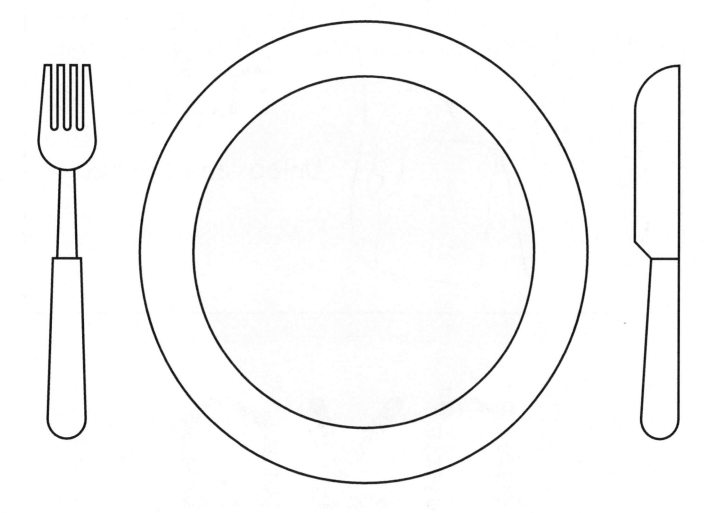

✶ Matzah ✶

The Hebrew word for unleavened bread is matzah. Matzah is a type of bread made from flour and water. Matzah is eaten during the Feast of Unleavened Bread.

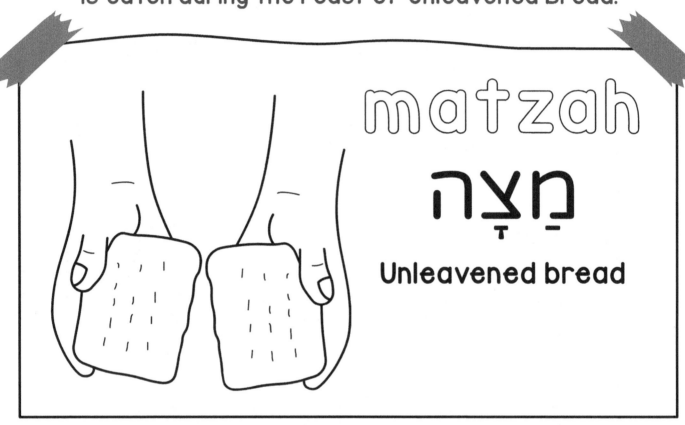

matzah

מַצָּה

Unleavened bread

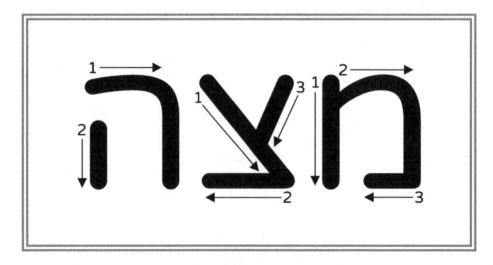

Let's write!

Practice writing this Hebrew word on the lines below.

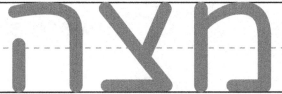

Try this on your own.
Remember that Hebrew is read from RIGHT to LEFT.

Yah's plan for
Israel

The Hebrews
were slaves in

Egypt

Yah sent Moses
to help free His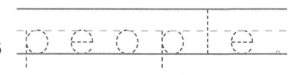

people

The Israelites lived in the

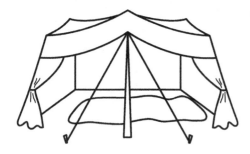

wilderness

for 40 years.

The Israelites' journey

The Israelites left Egypt and headed to the land of Canaan (the Promised Land). Connect the dots to see their journey from Egypt to the Jordan River.

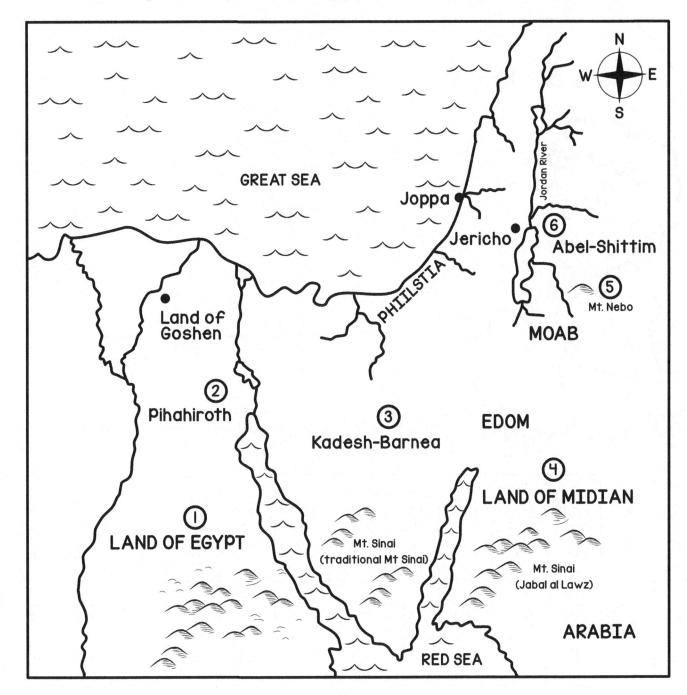

Who is our king?

Fill in the blanks using the chart below. What do you see?

Who is our king?

$\overline{25}$ $\overline{5}$ $\overline{19}$ $\overline{8}$ $\overline{21}$ $\overline{1}$

$\overline{9}$ $\overline{19}$ $\quad$ $\overline{20}$ $\overline{8}$ $\overline{5}$

$\overline{11}$ $\overline{9}$ $\overline{14}$ $\overline{7}$

A	B	C	D	E	F	G	H	I	J	K	L	M
1	2	3	4	5	6	7	8	9	10	11	12	13

N	O	P	Q	R	S	T	U	V	W	X	Y	Z
14	15	16	17	18	19	20	21	22	23	24	25	26

🌿 Preparation Day 🌿

Before Yeshua died, He ate a meal with His disciples.
He asked them to remember Him.

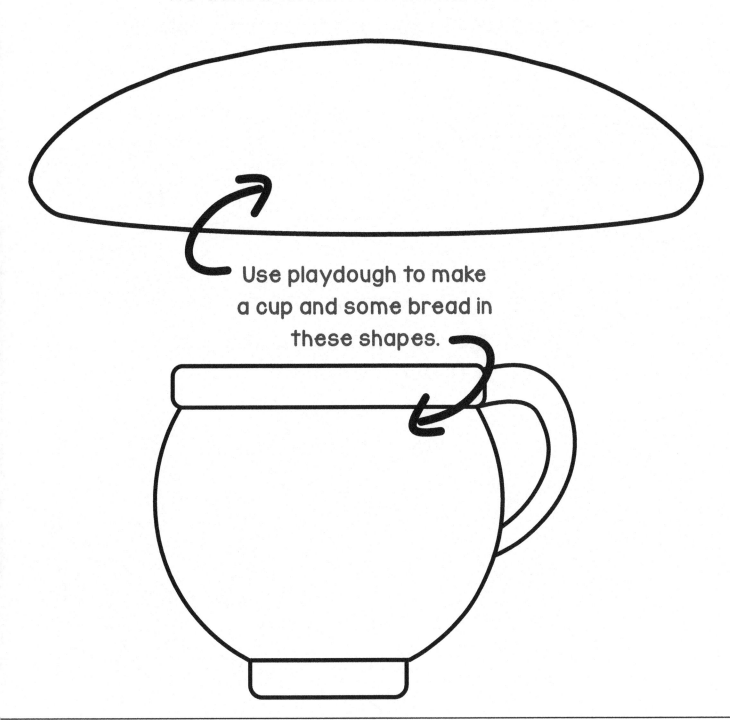

Use playdough to make
a cup and some bread in
these shapes.

A special meal

Educators: Read Mark 14:22-25 and John 13:21-30 with your children. Yeshua ate a meal with His disciples. Which disciple went out to betray Yeshua?

What did the men eat and drink?
Draw their meal.

🌿 The twelve disciples 🌿

Yeshua had twelve disciples.
They ate a meal with Him in an Upper Room in Jerusalem.
Can you count to 12? Count the boxes and write
the correct number in an empty box below.

Bartholomew	James **2**	Andrew **3**	Judas
Peter	John	Thomas **7**	James
Philip **9**	Matthew	Jude **11**	Simon

🌿 Garden of Gethsemane 🌿

Yeshua prayed in the garden of Gethsemane.
While he prayed, three disciples (Peter, James, and John)
fell asleep. Draw Yeshua and the disciples in the garden.

 What is a disciple?

Yeshua had twelve disciples. A disciple is someone
who follows Yeshua and does what He says.
How do you obey Him? Color part of the
foot each day as you behave like Yeshua.

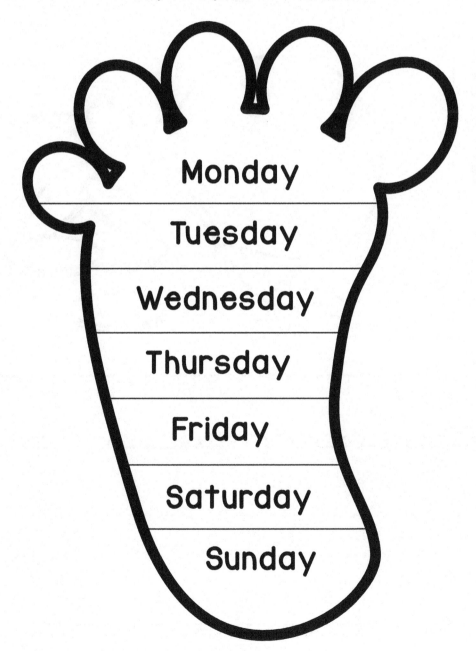

Monday

Tuesday

Wednesday

Thursday

Friday

Saturday

Sunday

The number One

One of the disciples betrayed Yeshua. His name was Judas.
He told the priests where to find Yeshua. The priests gave
Judas 30 pieces of silver. Write the number 1. Color the picture.

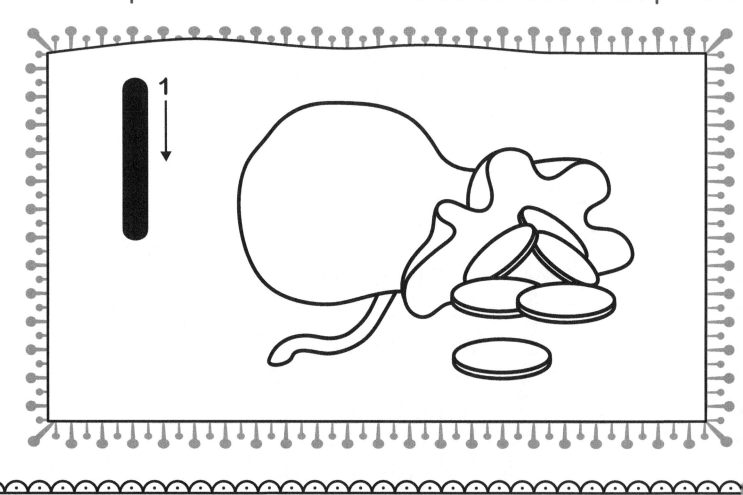

P is for Pilate

Pilate was the Roman governor. He sent Yeshua to die at Golgotha. Trace the letters and words. Color the picture.

P is for Pilate

Y is for Yeshua

Yeshua is the name of our Messiah.
Trace the letters. Color the picture.

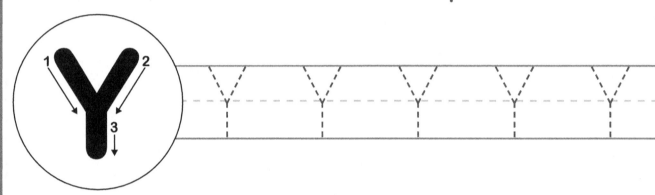

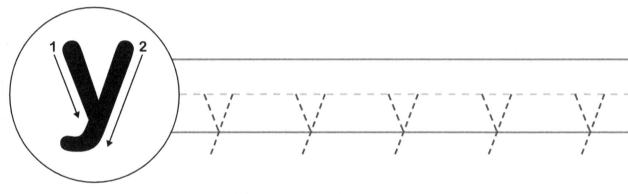

 Trace the letter Y

 Color the crown

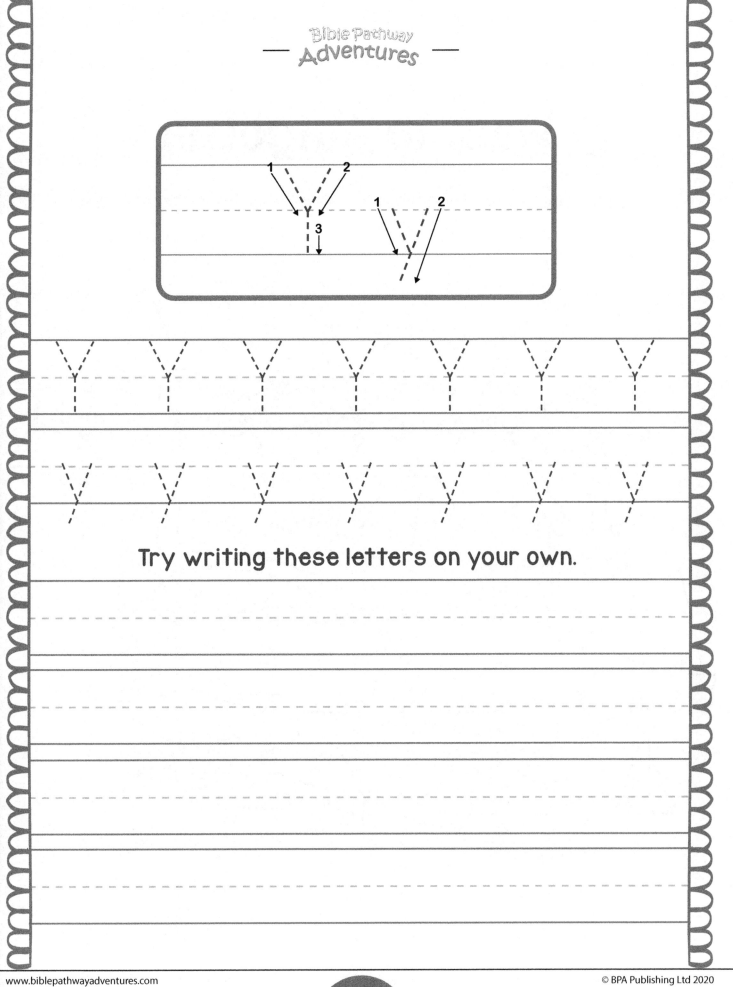

Try writing these letters on your own.

Walk to Golgotha

A man named Simon carried Yeshua's crossbeam to Golgotha. Help Simon find his way to Golgotha.

Bake a crown of thorns

Yeshua wore a crown of thorns on the cross.
Bake your own crown of thorns to remember our king.

INGREDIENTS
4 cups of flour
I cup of salt
Warm water to moisten the dough
Wooden toothpicks

METHOD
Preheat your oven to 350 F.
Combine the flour and salt in a large bowl.
Add enough water to make the dough sticky.
Mold the clay into three strands of dough.
Braid the dough and form a circle.
Bake in the oven at 350 F for 30 minutes, or until hard and dry.
Remove from oven.
When cool, place wooden toothpicks (thorns) in crown.

❧ Let's Trace ❧

The soldiers nailed Yeshua's wrists and ankles to two pieces of wood. These two pieces of wood formed a cross. Trace the lines to draw a cross.

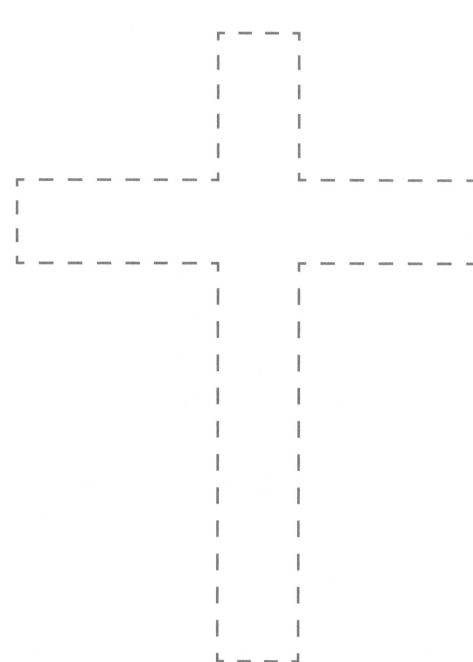

✿ Parts of a lamb ✿

The ancient Israelites ate lamb and bitter herbs
for the first Passover meal (Exodus 12:8).
Can you name the parts of a lamb?

ear

eye

mouth

feet

leg

❧ Trace the Words ❧

Color the pictures.

I am clean!

Yah wants us to eat 'clean' animals (Leviticus 11).
A lamb is a clean animal. Trace the words. Color the picture.

I am a lamb

Can you eat me?

🌿 What's my sound? 🌿

The word 'Passover' starts with the letter P.
Circle and color the pictures that have
the same beginning sound as Passover.

pumpkin

pajamas

cow

pizza

tree

The Passover

Find and circle each of the words from the list below.

```
C U P H D L
M R L E O A
S C F R O M
Z K P B R B
B R E A D B
F E E T B D
```

HERB   FEET
CUP   LAMB
DOOR   BREAD

Feast of First Fruits

The Feast of Unleavened Bread was a busy time in Jerusalem. Thousands of people came to the city to keep the Feast for seven days. Some slept in Jerusalem, while others stayed in nearby villages or in tents around the city.

During this Feast, there is an Appointed Time called First Fruits. This day falls on the day after the Sabbath during the Feast of Unleavened Bread. In ancient Israel, the High Priest would wave the first sheaf of barley before Yah at the temple on this day.

Did you know that Yeshua rose from the grave on the Feast of First Fruits? This is why Paul the Apostle wrote that He was the 'first fruits of those who have fallen asleep.'

Color the barley!

"Yeshua has been raised from the dead, the firstfruits of those who have fallen asleep."
(1 Corinthians 15:20)

🌿 A Roman soldier 🌿

After Yeshua was put inside a tomb, Roman soldiers
stood outside to make sure no one went in or out.
Color the picture.

🌿 Angel of God 🌿

An angel came down from heaven and opened the tomb. Connect the dots to show the picture.

🌿 He is Risen! 🌿

Yeshua rose from the dead on the Feast of First Fruits.
Trace the circles. Color the tomb.

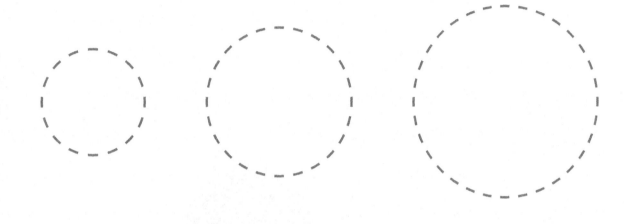

Yeshua is risen!

Draw Mary at Yeshua's tomb to complete the picture.

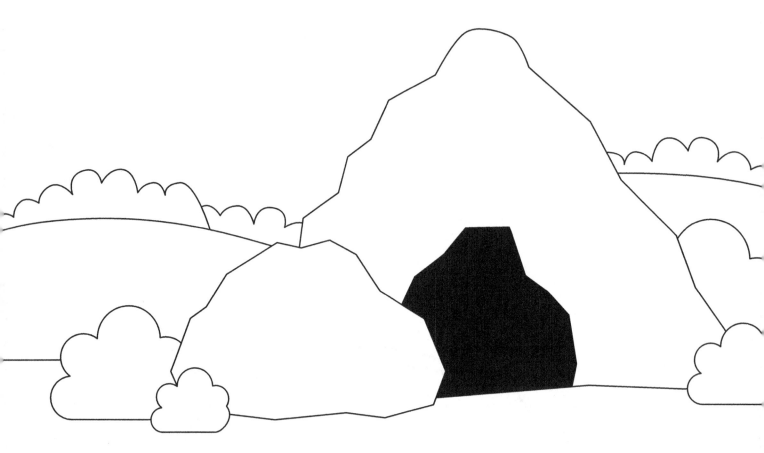

The number two

Two women saw Yeshua outside the tomb.
They were Mary Magdalene and Mary, mother of James.
Write the number 2. Color the pictures.

The High Priest

Color the hat white. Color the robe blue.

 He is Risen!

Find and circle each of the words from the list below.

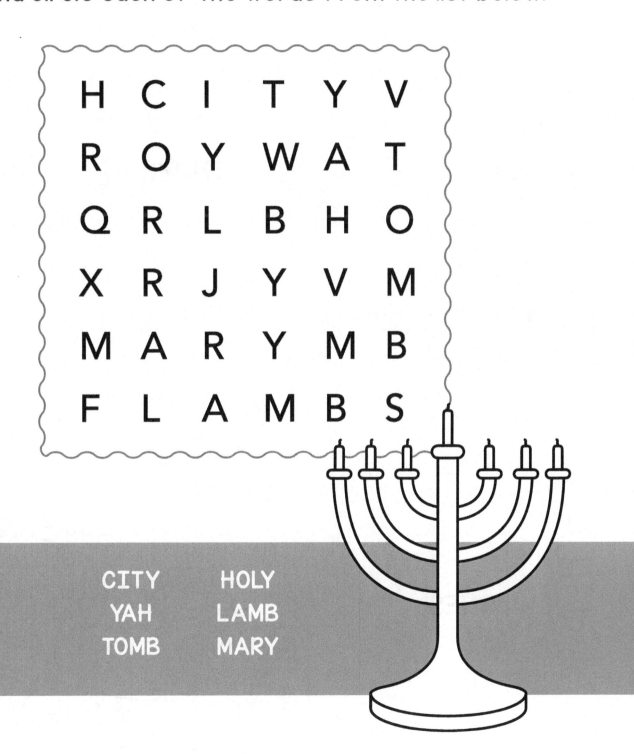

```
H  C  I  T  Y  V
R  O  Y  W  A  T
Q  R  L  B  H  O
X  R  J  Y  V  M
M  A  R  Y  M  B
F  L  A  M  B  S
```

CITY	HOLY
YAH	LAMB
TOMB	MARY

Days of the Week

Yeshua rose from the grave sometime after sunset
on Saturday and before sunrise on Sunday.
Fill in the letters to write the days of the week.

SUN D A Y   THURS __ __ __

MON __ __ __   FRI __ __ __

TUES __ __ __   SATUR __ __ __

WEDNES __ __ __ __

three

Yeshua was in the grave for three days and three nights.

3 3 3 3 3 3 3

Write the number three in the boxes below.

How many fingers are there?

Who came to the tomb to see Yeshua?

....

✴ Bikkurim ✴

The Hebrew word for Feast of First Fruits is Bikkurim.
Yeshua rose from the grave on this day. Our king is alive!

Bikkurim

בִּכּוּרִים

First Fruits

Let's write!

Practice writing this Hebrew word on the lines below.

בּיכורים

Try this on your own.
Remember that Hebrew is read from RIGHT to LEFT.

"He is Risen just as He Said."

(Matthew 28:6)

What's my sound?

The word 'disciple' starts with the letter D. Circle and color the pictures that have the same beginning sound as disciple.

cake

hat

dress

dog

donkey

🌿 Go to Galilee! 🌿

Yeshua told His disciples to go to Galilee. Connect the dots to help the disciples get to the Sea of Galilee.

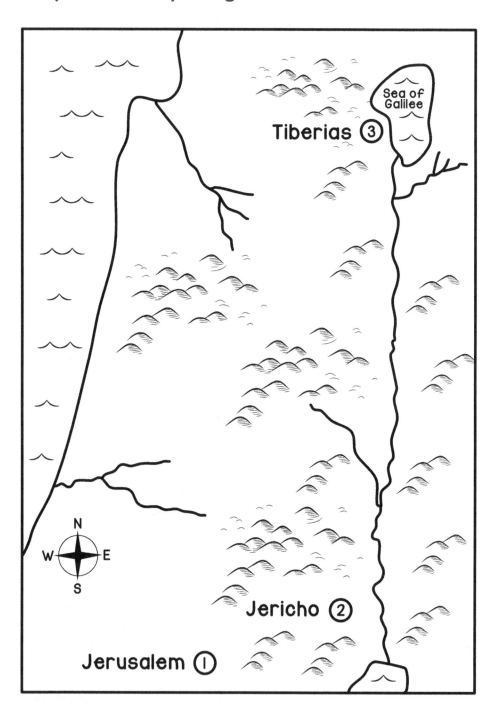

Shavu'ot - Day of Pentecost

Shavu'ot (the Day of Pentecost) is one of Yah's Feasts. When Yeshua was alive, men of Israel came to Jerusalem from different countries to celebrate this important Feast.

Shavu'ot is also the time when people remember how Yah gave the children of Israel the commandments (Torah) on Mount Sinai.

Peter and the disciples were in Jerusalem for Shavu'ot when they saw something that looked like flames of fire. That day, many men were able to understand what the disciples were saying in their own language. Some people think these men were of the ten tribes of Israel scattered abroad. Just like the disciples, they had come to Jerusalem to celebrate Shavu'ot.

Color the commandments!

🌿 Men of Israel 🌿

Trace along the lines to help the men of Israel
make their way to Jerusalem.

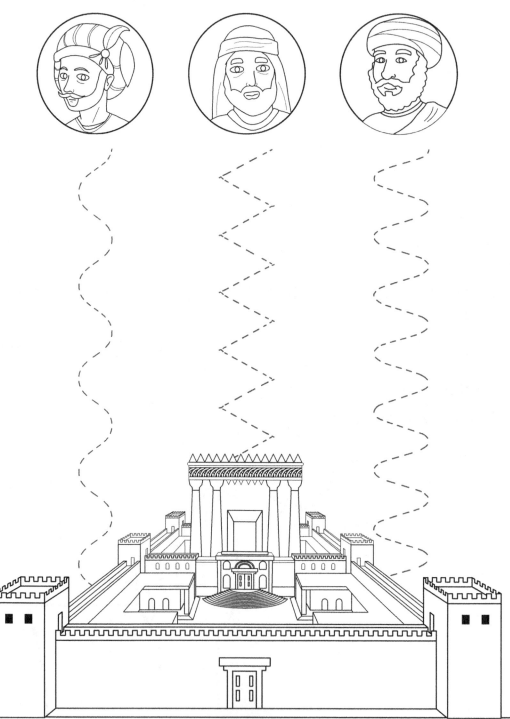

How did the Israelites travel?

Color the objects and animals that take you
from one place to another.

ark

donkey

camel

ship

giraffe

fish

elephant

🌿 The Israelites 🌿

Israelites came from many places to celebrate
Shavu'ot. Draw an arrow from each place to Jerusalem.

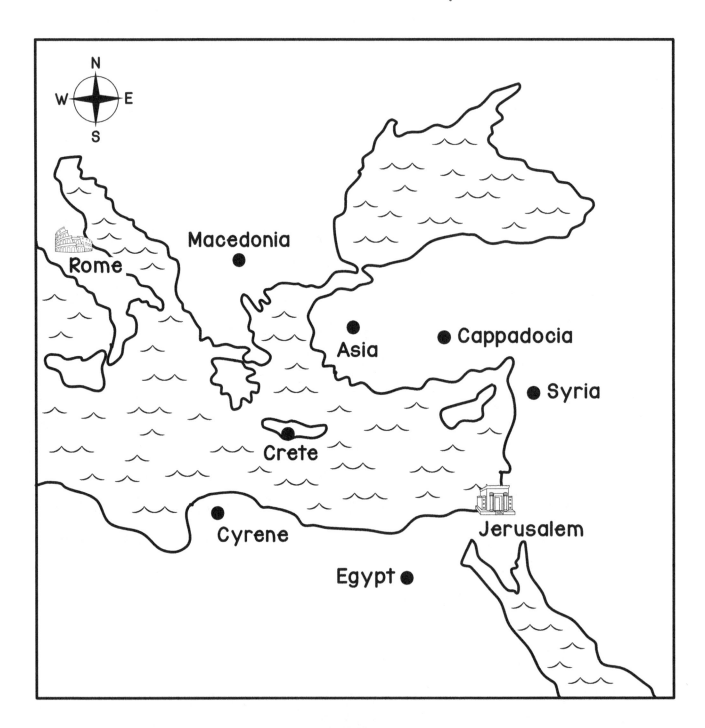

🌿 Twelve tribes of Israel 🌿

The High Priest at the temple wore a breastplate
with twelve stones; one for each tribe of Israel.
Color the picture.

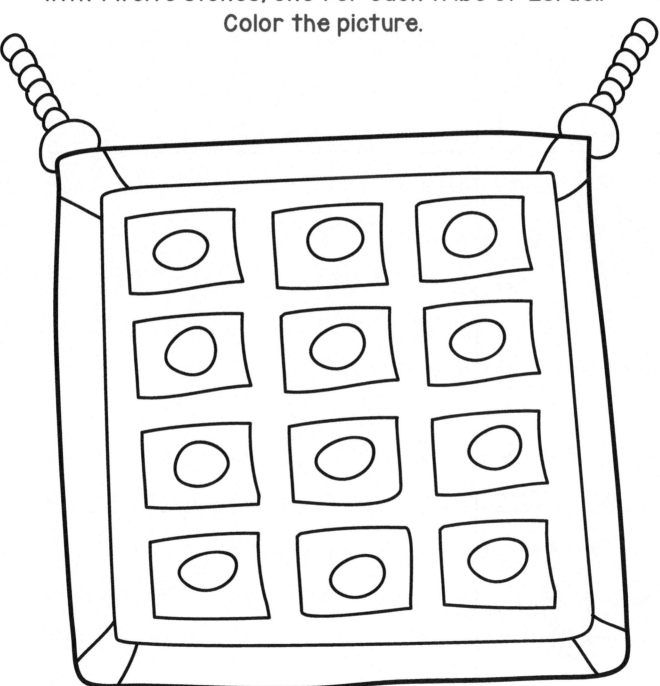

🌿 Trace the Words 🌿

Color the pictures.

fire

wind

Yah

temple

Peter the disciple

Peter was a disciple. He spoke to the men of Israel on Shavu'ot. Connect the dots to see the picture.

W is for wind

On Shavu'ot, the disciples heard a sound like
the blowing of wind. Trace the letters and words.
Color the picture.

w is for wind

✿ I spy! ✿

Color the same objects a single color. Then count each type of object and write the number on the label.

The Ten Commandments

🌿 Shavu'ot 🌿

Every year, the Israelites celebrated Shavu'ot.
Trace the word 'Shavu'ot'. Circle and color
the pictures that start with the letter 's'.

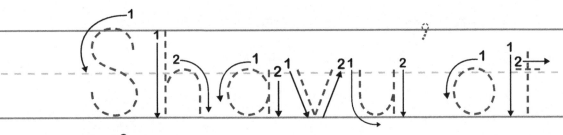

boat

 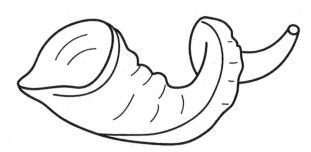

shofar

socks

tree

Yah spoke the ten commandments
to the Israelites.

10 10 10 10 10

Write the number ten in the boxes below.

How many fingers are there?

Do you obey the ten commandments?

❦ Dress like an Israelite ❦

The ancient Israelites wore clothing like tunics and robes. Let's make a tunic! Ask your parents to help you do this.

Instructions:

1. Parents - measure your child's body from elbow to elbow and knee to shoulder.
2. Find an old blanket or sheet as big as your child and fold it in half.
3. Cut a slit in the middle of the fold wide enough to fit their head.
4. Place the 'tunic' over their head. Tie a belt made from rope, ribbon, leather, or cloth around their waist.

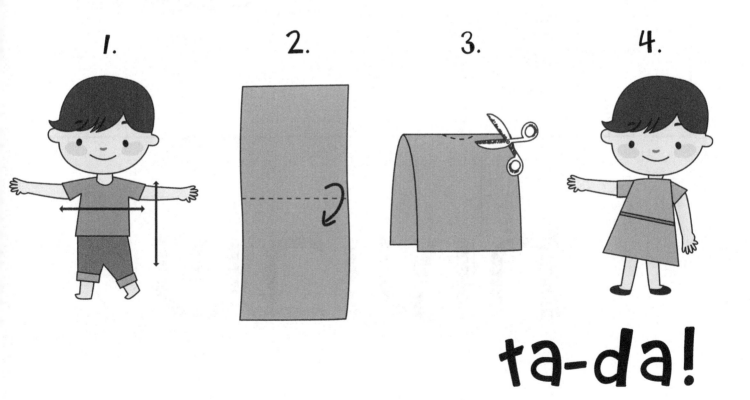

1.   2.   3.   4.

ta-da!

✶ Shavu'ot ✶

The Hebrew word for Day of Pentecost is Shavu'ot.
In ancient Israel, men from different places came
to Jerusalem to honor this Feast.

Shavu'ot

שָׁבוּעוֹת

Day of Pentecost

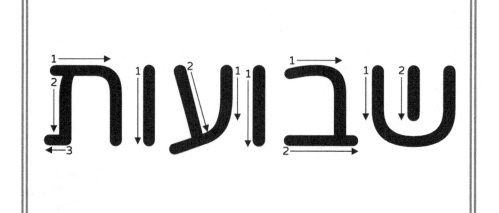

Let's write!

Practice writing this Hebrew word on the lines below.

שבועות

שבועות

Try this on your own.
Remember that Hebrew is read from RIGHT to LEFT.

"You will receive the gift of the Holy Spirit."

(Acts 2:38)

CRAFTS & PROJECTS

Make a Ten Plagues necklace

You will need:
1. Ten plagues pictures (see next pages)
2. Paint, felt pens, or crayons
3. Scissors or hole punch
4. Yarn or string

Instructions:

1. Have your children color the pictures of the ten plagues.
2. Cut out the pictures (children may need to help with this step).
3. Use a hole punch or scissors to create a hole in each of the circles.
4. String the circles with yarn or string to create a ten plagues necklace.

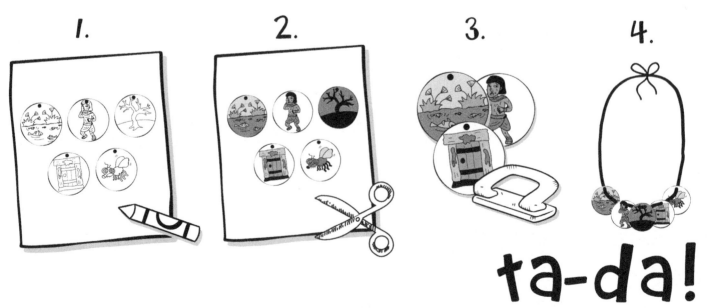

ta-da!

Passover flashcards

Cut out the flashcards and tape them
around your house or classroom!

egypt
5

yeshua
6

blood
7

matzah
8

🌿 Garden of Gethsemane 🌿

Yeshua spent time in the garden before He died.
The garden had many olive trees. Color the tree.
Cut out and paste together onto construction paper.

The Passover

Parents: discuss with your child how each picture relates to the Passover. Cut out a word at the bottom of the page. Place it next to the correct picture.

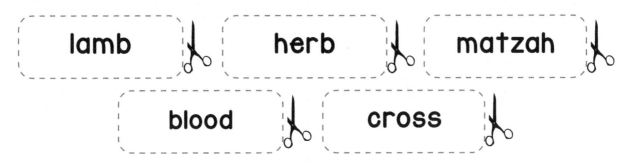

lamb   herb   matzah

blood   cross

The temple

On the Feast of First Fruits, the High Priest waved a sheaf of barley at the temple. Color and cut out the people and objects. Place them in the temple.

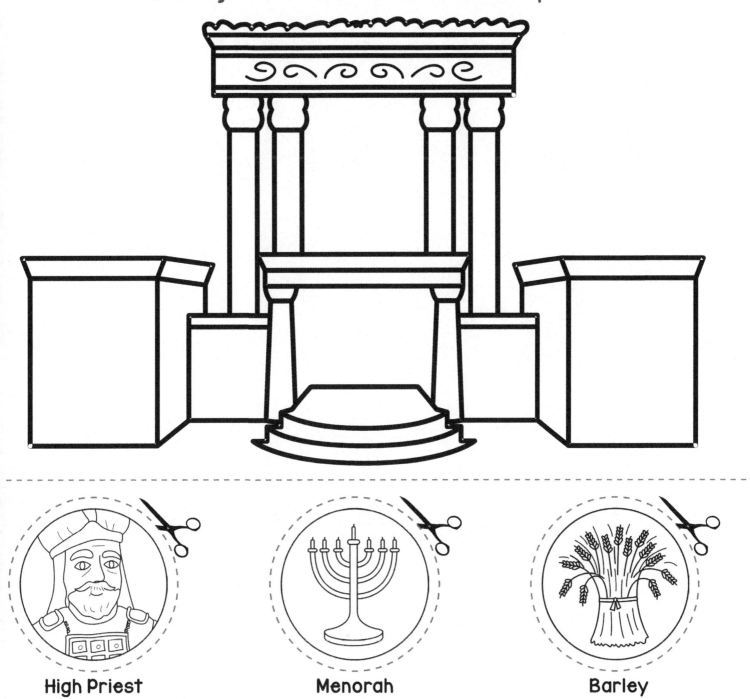

High Priest

Menorah

Barley

Resurrection paper plate craft

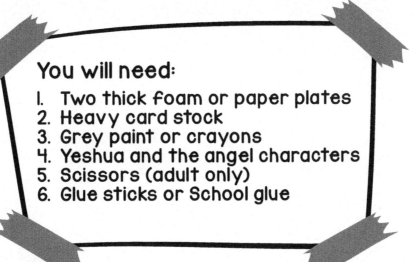

You will need:
1. Two thick foam or paper plates
2. Heavy card stock
3. Grey paint or crayons
4. Yeshua and the angel characters
5. Scissors (adult only)
6. Glue sticks or School glue

Instructions:

1. Cut out the Yeshua and angel templates. Make copies onto heavy card stock.
2. Cut the bottoms off both paper plates so they can stand up. Paint or color the paper plates grey. Remember to color the front and back!
3. While the paper plates are drying, color Yeshua and the angel.
4. Cut out a door on one paper plate. Glue both paper plates together to form a tomb. Glue Yeshua and the angel onto the tomb.

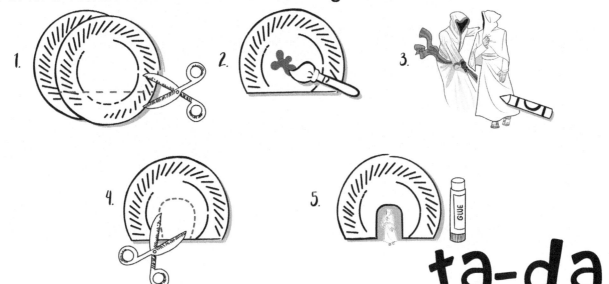

ta-da!

Bible characters: Yeshua and the angel.

Make an Appointed Times mobile

You will need:
1. Heavy card stock
2. Paint, felt pens, or crayons
3. String
4. Scissors (adult only)
5. Glue stick or tape
6. Wooden sticks

Instructions:

1. Ask your child to color the pictures inside each circle.
2. When your child has finished coloring, cut out the mobile pieces and glue onto heavy card stock.
3. Make a hole at the top of each mobile piece, string the pieces together, and attach to a piece of wood.

1.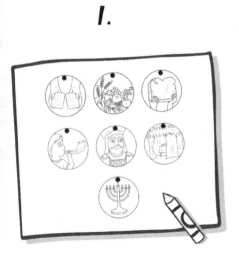

2.

3.

ta-da!

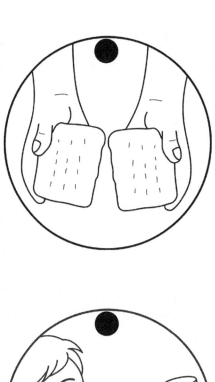

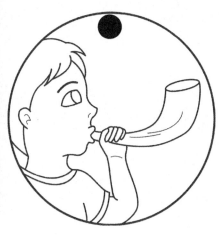

❧ The disciples ❧

Mary went into the city to tell the disciples that Yeshua was alive. Color and cut out Mary and the disciples. Place them in the house.

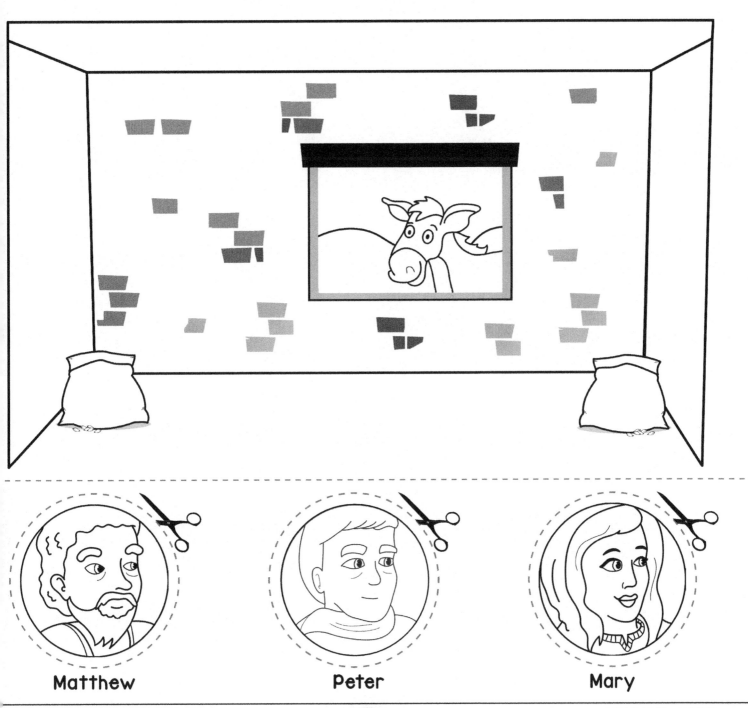

Matthew   Peter   Mary

🌿 Pentecost fact wheel 🌿

Cut out the templates. Insert a paper fastener through the middle of both templates and secure. Spin the wheel with your child and answer the questions.

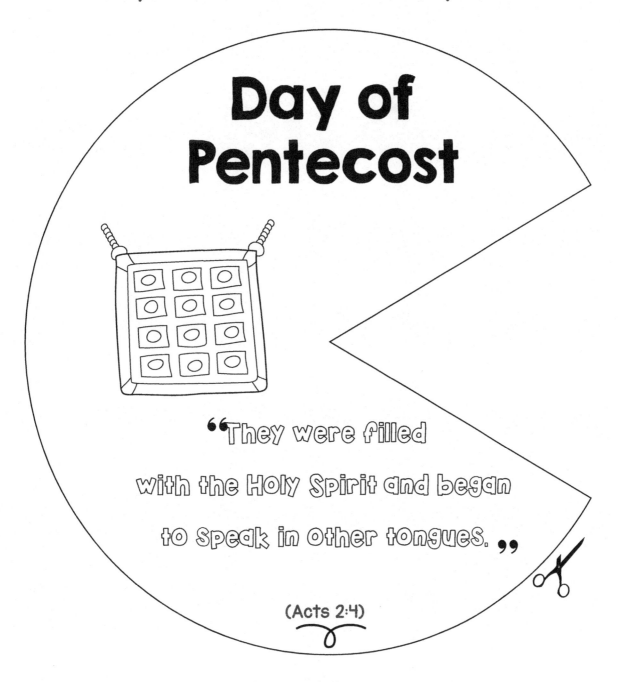

Day of Pentecost

"They were filled with the Holy Spirit and began to speak in other tongues."

(Acts 2:4)

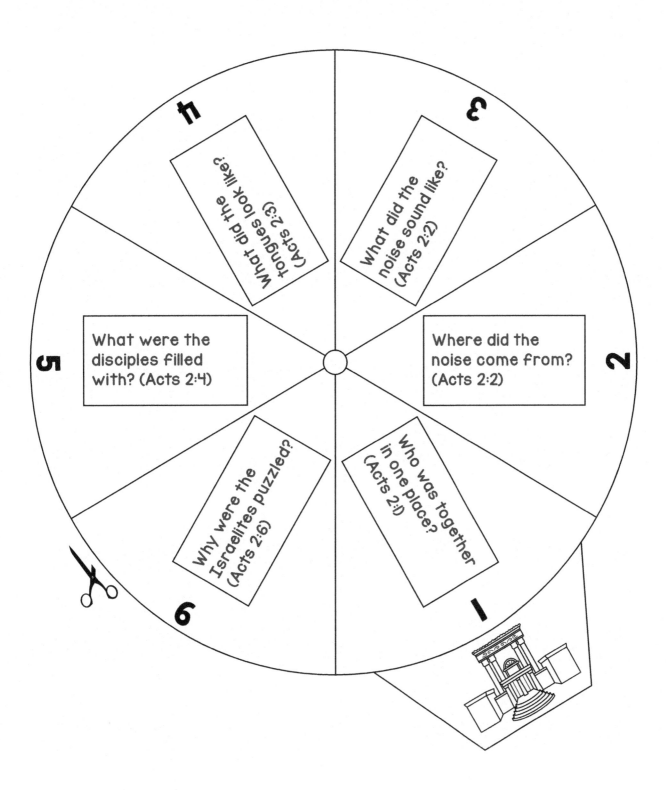

4

What did the tongues look like? (Acts 2:3)

3

What did the noise sound like? (Acts 2:2)

5

What were the disciples filled with? (Acts 2:4)

2

Where did the noise come from? (Acts 2:2)

6

Why were the Israelites puzzled? (Acts 2:6)

1

Who was together in one place? (Acts 2:1)

Shavu'ot flashcards

Color the flashcards. Cut out each flashcard and paste it onto a wooden stick. Can you retell the story of Shavu'ot (Pentecost) in Acts 1-2?

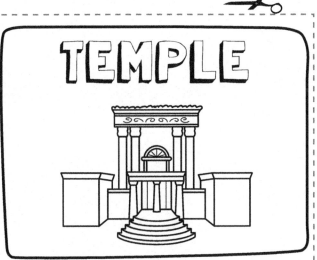

PETER

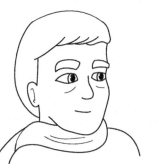

HOLY SPIRIT

YESHUA

HEAR

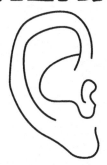

12 TRIBES

JERUSALEM

Help Moses climb Mount Sinai

You will need:
1. Paper plate (one for each child)
2. Paper fastener (one for each plate)
3. Paint, markers, or crayons
4. Scissors (adults-only)

Instructions:

1. Cut your paper plate in half.
2. Color your mountain grey using paint, markers or crayons. Draw green trees or leaves at the bottom of the plate.
3. Cut out the Moses template. Paste onto heavy card stock.
4. Insert the paper fastener into the bottom center of the paper plate. Push the fastener into the long end of the Moses template and secure. Now Moses can climb up and down Mount Sinai!

1.   **2.**   **3.**

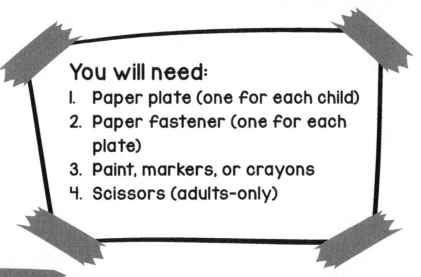

ta-da!

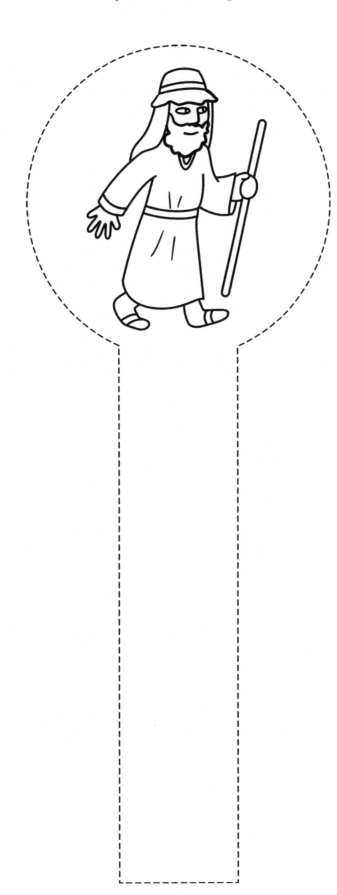

Discover more Activity Books!

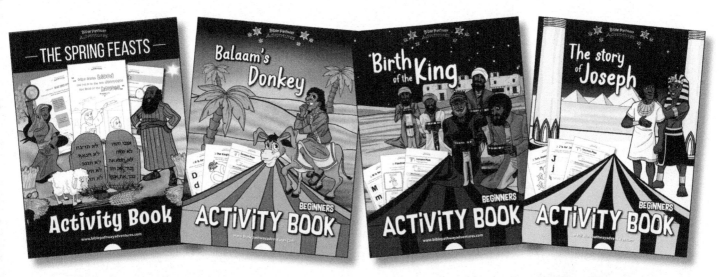

Available for purchase at www.biblepathwayadventures.com

INSTANT DOWNLOAD!

The Spring Feasts	The Spring Feasts Beginners
Balaam's Donkey	Moses Ten Plagues
Birth of the King	The Exodus
The Story of Joseph	The Story of Esther

Made in United States
Orlando, FL
01 May 2022

17388132R00065